S0-BOE-857

Essential Question
How do animal characters change familiar stories?

The Prince Who Could Fly

by Philippa Werry

illustrated by
Caroline Hu

A Visitor

Characters:
PRINCESS, MAID, KING, QUEEN, PRINCE/CANARY, WISE WOMAN, NURSE

Scene: *Inside the castle, the* **PRINCESS** *is looking out a window. The* **MAID** *comes in.*

MAID: Good morning, Princess. Would you like some breakfast?

Princess

PRINCESS: No, thanks.

MAID: (*looks out the window*) Here comes your father, the King, and his wife, the new Queen.

The **MAID** *leaves and returns with the* **KING** *and the* **QUEEN.**

KING: Good morning, daughter. You look tired. Are you okay?

QUEEN: (*frowning*) Don't be ridiculous. She looks fine!

2

PRINCESS: I'm all right, Father. I only wish I could live with you.

KING: Well, perhaps one day—

QUEEN: (*interrupts*) You live in a lovely castle. Why are you complaining?

PRINCESS: I get so frustrated living here. It's very lonely.

QUEEN: We visit you. Your maid takes care of you and keeps you company, too. Don't be selfish.

PRINCESS: It's boring here. All I do is sit by the window and stare at the <u>trees</u>.

QUEEN: (*impatiently*) You're safe in the castle.

KING: Yes, the forest is dangerous. There are wolves and other wild animals.

Language Detective	<u>Trees</u> is a plural noun. Find other plural nouns on this page.

PRINCESS: (*sighs*) I know, Father.

QUEEN: Lots of girls would love to live in a castle. Don't complain again, or I'll be very annoyed.

KING: (*to the* **QUEEN**) Can she come home with us?

QUEEN: Definitely not! I don't like her attitude.

The **KING** *and the* **QUEEN** *leave.*

MAID: The Queen is cranky today!

The **PRINCESS** *sighs.*

King

Queen

MAID: Her specialty is being mean. Why did the King marry her after your mother died?

PRINCESS: Maybe he was lonely. I wish she'd forget to lock the door. Then we could escape!

MAID: Here, lean on this cushion when you look out the window. You will be more comfortable.

PRINCESS: You're so kind to me. Thank you.

5

MAID: You deserve kindness. I'll make lunch.

*The **MAID** leaves. The **PRINCESS** leans on the cushion and looks out the window. The **PRINCE** comes and stops in front of the castle.*

PRINCE: I smell food cooking. (*yelling*) Hello?

PRINCESS: (*yelling*) Hello.

PRINCE: Hi. I thought the castle was empty. Do you live here now?

PRINCESS: Yes, I do.

PRINCE: Would you like to go for a ride on my horse?

PRINCESS: I'd love to go for a ride, but I'm not allowed to leave the castle.

PRINCE: Then, can I come in? I'm very thirsty.

PRINCESS: I'm sorry. The door is locked.

MAID: (*comes in with food*) Here's your lunch, Princess.

*The **PRINCESS** is talking to the **PRINCE**. The **MAID** puts the food down and goes away.*

STOP AND CHECK

Where does the Princess live? Who lives with her?

The Special Book

Scene: *The* **PRINCESS** *is looking out the window.*

MAID: You look cheerful this morning.

PRINCESS: I'm hoping the Prince will come back today. (*hears a horse coming*) Here he comes!

PRINCE: (*shouting*) Good morning!

PRINCESS: Good morning. It's a beautiful day. I'm sorry I can't go riding with you.

PRINCE: At least we can keep each other company.

There is the sound of knocking from another part of the castle.

Prince

MAID: Do you hear knocking?

The **PRINCE** *and the* **PRINCESS** *are busy talking and don't answer.*

castle

In Other Words talk, spend time together. En español, *keep each other company* quiere decir *nos hacemos compañia*.

7

MAID: I'll be back. (*goes downstairs. The* **WISE WOMAN** *is tapping at a window*) Hello?

WISE WOMAN: I am the Wise Woman of the Forest.

MAID: (*opens window*) How can I help you?

WISE WOMAN: I'm here to help the Prince and the Princess.

MAID: How will you do that? Do you have a <u>key</u> to the castle?

WISE WOMAN: No, but I have a special book for the Princess. (*She gives the* **MAID** *the book through the window.*) Tell her to turn the pages.

MAID: What do you mean?

WISE WOMAN: (*talking to herself as she walks away*) Turn them this way, then turn them that way.

The **MAID** *goes upstairs with the book.*

Language Detective	<u>Key</u> is a singular noun. Find other singular nouns on this page.

MAID: Excuse me, Princess. A woman told me to give this book to you.

The **MAID** *gives the book to the* **PRINCESS**.

MAID: She said you have to turn the pages this way, then turn them that way.

PRINCESS: (*turns the pages forward*) Nothing happens. I feel a little foolish. (*looks out window*) Where did the Prince go?

A yellow canary flies in through the window.

MAID: Quick! Turn the pages the other way.

The **PRINCESS** *turns the pages back. The yellow canary changes into the* **PRINCE**.

PRINCE: (*standing next to the* **PRINCESS**) Princess, what happened?

PRINCESS: It's this special book. When I turned the pages, you changed into a canary and flew up here. Now we can spend time together.

PRINCE: That's wonderful! But, I need to go home now. I'll come back as soon as I can.

The **PRINCESS** *turns the pages forward. The* **PRINCE** *changes into a canary and flies to the ground. The* **PRINCESS** *turns the pages back, and the canary changes into the* **PRINCE**.

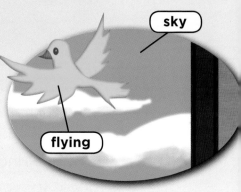

PRINCE: Good-bye! I'll be back soon!

STOP AND CHECK

How did the Wise Woman help the Prince and Princess?

A Cure

Scene: *The* **PRINCESS** *sits by the window smiling. The* **QUEEN** *arrives.*

QUEEN: *(suspiciously)* You look cheerful today.

PRINCESS: Thank you, Your Majesty.

QUEEN: Why are you in such a good mood?

PRINCESS: It's a beautiful day.

QUEEN: *(to herself)* Something strange is going on. *(to the* **PRINCESS***)* Go and get me a drink.

PRINCESS: Yes, Your Majesty. *(leaves the room)*

QUEEN: *(takes sharp pins from her hair)* I'll put these pins in the cushion. The Princess will be surprised when she leans on it. *(The* **PRINCESS** *comes back with a glass of water.)* I'm not thirsty anymore. I have to go. Good-bye.

The **QUEEN** *leaves. Then the* **MAID** *comes in.*

MAID: The Prince is here.

> **In Other Words** happening. En español, *going on* quiere decir *está pasando.*

11

PRINCE: *(calling up to the window)* Princess?

PRINCESS: Hello. Let me get the book.

The **MAID** *gives the* **PRINCESS** *the book. The* **PRINCESS** *turns the pages forward. The canary flies to the window and lands on the cushion. The canary is hurt by the pins.*

MAID: The canary is hurt! He's flying back down to the ground. Quick, turn the pages back.

The **PRINCESS** *turns the pages back. The canary changes into the* **PRINCE**. *He is hurt. He gets on his horse and rides away.*

PRINCESS: I must find out if he's okay. But the door is locked.

MAID: Let's tear up the sheets on the bed and make a rope.

crown

horse

rein

The **PRINCESS** *and the* **MAID** *tear the sheets.*

MAID: Hold on to the sheets. I'll lower you down.

PRINCESS: Will you be okay? Imagine the commotion when the Queen finds I'm not here.

MAID: Don't worry about me. I want to see the expression on the Queen's face when she discovers you're gone.

The **MAID** *helps the* **PRINCESS** *climb down.*

PRINCESS: I don't know how to find the Prince.

The **WISE WOMAN** *steps out of the forest.*

WISE WOMAN: Follow the river to the palace. Take this. (*She hands the* **PRINCESS** *some medicine.*) The Prince is hurt, but the medicine will save him.

PRINCESS: Thank you!

The **PRINCESS** *runs through the forest.*

The **PRINCESS** *arrives at the palace. A* **NURSE** *leads her to the* **PRINCE**. *The* **PRINCE** *is asleep. He looks sick.*

PRINCESS: This medicine will cure the Prince.

The **PRINCESS** *gives the medicine to the* **NURSE**. *The* **NURSE** *rubs the medicine on the* **PRINCE**. *The* **PRINCE** *opens his eyes.*

PRINCESS: Hello, Prince. Do you know who I am?

PRINCE: Of course. You are as familiar to me as my own heart. How did you get here?

PRINCESS: I followed the river ... then I followed my heart.

STOP AND CHECK

How did the Princess help the Prince?

Respond to Reading

Summarize

Use important details to summarize *The Prince Who Could Fly*. Your graphic organizer may help you.

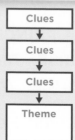

Text Evidence

1. What text features tell you that this is a drama? **GENRE**

2. How does the prince help the princess? **THEME**

3. Find the word *safe* on page 3. What is the meaning of *safe*? Use the context clues to help you figure out the meaning. Find the antonym on the same page. **SYNONYMS AND ANTONYMS**

4. Write about the message the author communicates by having the princess go to help the prince. **WRITE ABOUT READING**

Compare Texts

Read a story about an animal who solves a mystery.

The Mystery of the Spotted Dogs

"Where are you going, Mrs. Marjoram?" the animals asked.

"I want to buy a Dalmatian puppy," Mrs. Marjoram said.

At that moment, Detective Dog woke up from a dream. "What's going on?" Detective Dog asked.

"Mrs. Marjoram wants to buy a Dalmatian puppy," Tabitha Cat replied.

Mrs. Marjoram told Detective Dog the price for the puppy.

"That's *very* expensive. I should go with you," Detective Dog said.

The animals wanted to go, too. Sheep, Goose, Duck, Pig, and Cat all got in the van.

Soon they arrived at a small farm.

Mrs. Marjoram knocked on the door. A man opened it.

"We've come to see your puppies," Mrs. Marjoram said.

The man took them to the barn and showed them the puppies.

"They are cute!" Goose said.

"So little! So many spots!" Pig said.

"How old are they?" Detective Dog asked the man.

"Three days old," the man said.

"Are they genuine Dalmatian puppies?" Detective Dog asked.

"Yes," the man said. He pointed to the spots on the puppies.

"Mrs. Marjoram, don't buy the puppies. They aren't genuine Dalmatians," Detective Dog said.

"How do you know?" Mrs. Marjoram asked.

"Dalmatian puppies are born without spots. These puppies are three days old, and they already have spots. Look closely. You will see the spots have been painted on the puppies. The man is lying," said Detective Dog.

"Detective Dog, I'm glad you came with me today," Mrs. Marjoram said.

Make Connections

How does Detective Dog help Mrs. Marjoram? **ESSENTIAL QUESTION**

How is the Wise Woman in *The Prince Who Could Fly* similar to Detective Dog in *The Mystery of the Spotted Dogs*? **TEXT TO TEXT**

Focus on Genre

Dramas Dramas are stories that are performed for an audience. The text is mostly dialogue, and there are stage directions that describe what the characters do. Dramas have scenes instead of chapters.

Read and Find In *The Prince Who Could Fly*, the stage directions are in italics. The directions tell the actors where the scene is set and what the characters do. In the dialogue, the name of the character appears first. A colon (:) separates the character's name from the words the character speaks.

Your Turn

Turn to page 6. With a partner, find the stage directions that tell what the characters do.

Reread pages 2–3. With a partner, write sentences to describe the Princess, the King, and the Queen. Describe where the scene takes place and how each character feels.